OPEN-MOUTHED

OPEN-MOUTHED

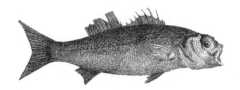

FOOD POEMS

JAMES CROWDEN ALAN PEACOCK

LAWRENCE SAIL ELISABETH ROWE

PROSPECT BOOKS

2006

First published in Great Britain in 2006 by Prospect Books, Allaleigh House, Blackawton, Totnes, Devon TQ9 7DL.

ISBN 1-903018-49-8

Typeset by Tom Jaine.
Printed in Great Britain by Kingfisher Print, Totnes, Devon.

Foreword

Here, in *Open-mouthed*, the reader can find a rich *à la carte* menu of poems, some *al dente*, others *al fresco*, succulent morsels plucked from hedgerows and kitchens at home and abroad. But why have four poets from Devon come together to create a collection of poems about food, some of them light-hearted, some more serious? For the pleasure of it, no doubt, but also to raise money for the Dartington 'Ways With Words' literary festival, specifically in order to help fund a bursary scheme enabling young students to attend the festival, an experience with the potential to broaden their interests and awaken their intellects.

This culinary gang of four also hopes to make these poems available to a wider audience, particularly now that the resurgent interest in local food is flavour of the month. Combining this with poetry seems an obvious step forward, to educate and enliven our tastes.

So here you will find, for instance, Cornish earlies alongside borscht, pistachios and mussels, wild mushrooms mixing with a hostess trolley, artichokes and alphabet soups, tripe an' cow 'eels, sad cake and sloes, trout hatcheries, mushy peas, mammoths and the Meat Commission: dishes to suit all tastes. And, above all, these poems are fun.

CAROL TREWIN
FOOD EDITOR, *Western Morning News*
April 2006

Acknowledgements

We are very grateful to Tom Jaine of Prospect books for agreeing to publish this collection.

We are also grateful to Bloodaxe Books for allowing us to reproduce some of Lawrence Sail's poems from previous collections: 'Alphabet Soup'; 'In the Trout Hatchery'; 'Eating Maize'; 'Paysages Moralisés 2'; 'The Meat Commission, Kenya' from *Out of Land: New & Selected Poems*, 1992. 'Fish Magic' and 'Pistachios and Mussels' from *Building into Air*, 1995. 'Sloes'; 'Valentine's Night in the Supermarket' (from the sequence 'Out of Silence') from *The World Returning*, 2002. 'Sparrowgrass'; 'White Peach'; 'Feeding the Dolls' from *Eye-Baby*, 2006.

We are grateful for permission to reproduce Elisabeth Rowe's poem 'The Marrow' from *Surface Tension*, published by Peterloo Poets, 2003.

'Apple Haiku' by James Crowden was first published in *Cider – the Forgotten Miracle*, published by Cyder Press 2 in 1999. 'Burrow Hill Cider Farm' was first published in this form in *In Time of Flood*, The Parrett Trail Partnership 1996. 'Hard Cheese – Somerset' first appeared in *Petits Propos Culinaires* 70, 2002.

Contents

Cornish Earlies

Deliciously dirty, dig for victory
Tubers m' hansum, multiplied again and again
Golden nuggets surfacing from the depths

Of the light, rich, hand picked Penwith soil,
Young skin, smooth and peeling,
Scrubbed clean, brought to heel with mint

And boiling water, simmered,
Yellow grape-shot bursting forth
In clouds of steam, drained and tipped out

On the kitchen table, smeared all over,
Cornish butter, glazed, running at the edges
Fruits of the earth, bulging and succulent.

Take your pick. The Golden Mile
Melts in the mouth, a seaward glance.
First crop, first light. The pilchard awaits.

JC

Alphabet Soup

The sunken letters keep their options,
scarcely evolved in a soapy broth
where the last word on any subject
melts to an anagram of moonshine,
literal truth.

No given usage quite wears them out:
consumed, they might be the sacrament
of pride swallowed – or, stirred, resettle
oh in omens, telling the future
in new last words.

Innocent as messengers they stand
by, are only bearers of the word –
already looking elsewhere, as we
try to break the rosy seals, to get
at real meaning.

LS

Globe Artichoke

Is it a thistle? A mallet? A rattle? No!
It's a 'choke! A veg., un vrai artichaut,
straight from the fields of Morlaix and Saint Pol,
a heavy-headed, heavy-handled globe
that ought to come with clear instructions for use
on what to eat, what not, and how to cook.
They come in various models (cone-shaped, violet);
but back to our globe; this is what to do.

Click off the petals, one by one, till you come
to paler yellow and more tender leaves.
Remove the fluffy choke. Rub lemon in
so it won't discolour, and bake for half an hour.
Dip leaves in melted butter or vinaigrette,
then scrape the tender flesh off with your teeth.
You'll be left with the base, or heart; a rich reward
for all the grief. This is the best part yet.
Dip; savour; indulge yourself. Relief!

AP

Borscht

Red and brown, muddy
Hand grenades
That have not gone off.
Pull the pin out
Top and tail them
Scrub and grate,
Bleed into a pan,
Careful not to loose
The precious dye.
Simmer, shake, stir and prod
Feed the leaves to the nearest rabbit.
Inexplicable, the earthy smell
Beetroot on parade,
Beating out its own time
A texture which you wish
To keep sacred.
Add an onion or two,
Butternut Squash
If you like,
A mortar bomb
Cut into small pieces,
Dash of cider, vinegar
Garlic and ham stock,
Bacon, sugar, bay
Lemon, parsley, dill.
Sour cream

The white knob floating in
A sea of reddish purple
The Polish navy
On manoeuvres
Moored to a solid wharf,
Chunks of rye bread.

                                        JC

Asparagus

Straight up
like a gift of special pencils tied with ribbon;
the first taste of summer
for a two month season.

Tipped
and steamed, creamed or griddled Jamie style
with olive oil, butter and pepper,
every chef's favourite.

Some
will say it tastes like tough, weird grass,
preferring frozen peas
with a crozzled steak.

But most
have never even known the taste of green;
waiting, expecting nothing
under shadeless sun.

What energy
And water, what air-miles, year after year,
to guarantee such luxuries,
while pickers have no garden, home, or school,
not even a pencil.
Straight up.   AP

A la Carte

Let me prepare for you
Cornfed carp with a coulis of saffron marmalade
Filo parcel of snails in sorrel sauce

Let me bring to your table
Caribbean caviar with galette of pistachio and endive
Ballottine of quail with mozzarella

Consider tonight's special
Rack of pigeon with Roquefort and chargrilled pinenuts
Red mullet in a maple syrup marinade

And for the sweet tooth
Quenelles of passion fruit parfait with parmesan shavings
Beetroot sorbet in a spun sugar basket

Don't come here to eat
If you don't know your bourride from your bouillabaisse
Don't cry for me, fettucine

This is my philosophy:
Recipes are like dogs, they can smell fear; saucepans have
    ears
Knives have a way of cutting

                                                        ER

Sparrowgrass FOR HELEN

Butter-wet, lickerous,
tender tongue-tie,
wilt-headed fasces,
maytime mouth-melt,
work of the fingers,
lips and tongue,
more a bird
in hand than in the bush –
and offering a way
to recover a baby's
unashamed delight,
afterwards, by sucking
each finger clean.

LS

Dartmouth Crab

Walks sideways onto your plate
Sandwiched between two trawlers of bread
And a pot or two of salt and pepper over the side
In any weather hauled to the surface

Harvest of rocks and reefs
The pincer movement of the waitresses
Insures you get good service
Claws and belly up. A squirt of lemon,

A dash across the bottom.
Brown sides cave in, keel hauled.
Moored up for the afternoon
The shell suit, discarded.

JC

Nine Dabs

The boy waits on the harbour wall,
dangling his clogs over a sheen
of sheltered water, eyeing the dangerous
glitter of dark blue open sea.

The old man counts silver coins
for silver fish, chapped hands
glinting with tiny scales.
The dabs die roughly: gills

still stubbornly gaping, tails
lashing the bag all the way home.
The boy slides them into stainless
steel where light slippery as life

shifts among their orange, green
and grey undimmed sea dazzle.

ER

Fast Food – Low Tide

Samphire and marsh mutton
Dulce and glasswort
Sloke and carrageen

Laver, green and purple
Rich delicacies plucked
And harvested from the sea shore

Such miracles provided
In time of fast, like glatting
The hunt for congers at low tide,

Amongst the rocks with dogs,
Stake fisheries and mud-horses
The shore prickly like a stickleback.

JC

In the Trout Hatchery

1

Superfluous now the upstream gravel
of redds cut clean, the drift of milt:
this river has no story, travels
a table's length, mouths into buckets
and spills away. Sky is a tilt
of dark and starless wood.
Conceived to order, these need no luck.

They harbour their plans. Beneath the skin,
black pips for eyes: each berry stores
enough to last two months of waiting.
As soft as ticks, pre-human, apart,
they glow with knowledge, calmly adoring
the quiet circles of time.
In time, they panic the human heart.

2

Black inches spate
beneath the wheel
which regulates
the fall of feed –
a printer's tray
of twitching marks

bumping and turning
through light and dark,
gold–eyed greed.

You gladly shift
your gaze to where
a few fish drift
calmly – one yaws
in rings, its spine
a rigid bend;
eyeless, another
comes to an end
blindly in jaws.

Between two fears
your mind demands
a choice: but here
in one long line
the equal water
shines and shines.

LS

Elvers

Thin filaments smelling of the North Atlantic
Prone to the Gulf Stream and spring tides
Are drawn by the moon

Into the clutches of man and boy,
Wriggling filaments that crawl to the sides
Of slimy rivers, rhynes and ditches

Glass eels, a rite of passage
For all concerned,
Translucent, pale and gelatinous,

Taoist delicacy, avowed aphrodisiac
Fry up gently in bacon fat
Break in an egg or two.

Scramble, stir and serve on toast
Chopped herbs, the elver cake
Very welcome in the hungry gap.

JC

Sea Bass

First catch your bass. Take one rowing boat,
This one was a Norwegian Rana, then take a beach
Launch the boat down the shingle, boards smeared
    with lard

Row carefully through the breaking waves
Lay a net below the cliffs, one you prepared earlier,
And standing up, pay the net out carefully

As if it was a washing line, tether at both ends
With anchors of your choice. Mark with buoys
And then return to shore, to the nearest pub.

Next morning, early, without disturbing inhabitants,
Row back out, and if you are very lucky there will be
Something in your net besides scad and sea weed.

That morning in the sunlight beneath the cliffs
A silver salver floating on the surface, untouched by
Gulls, caught by its fin and still alive, treading water,

Not one of those other silver ones, so we took it along
To the post office and weighed it up on their scales.
Nine pounds flapping. The deal done over the phone.

JC

Ling Turbot: the Fish Opera @ Newlyn Fish Market 6 am

Early morning scales glitter
Silver ingots hoisted from the deep
Shunted around, in boxes
At high speed, the bidding war
Ice like confetti
Scattered over the wet floor
Conger curled up asleep
Skate wings it, flying low,
Megrim sole, Lundy, Fastnet
Copper green mackerel,
Monkfish, nod and a wink
Bass, playing the sea's orchestra,
With a herring aid
Pilchard in need of salt,
Squid, inked out
Lobster clawing its way back
To find its Quadrille
Your plaice or mine ?
Gurnard's head
The chorus
Coley, Dab and Pollock
Mullet over,
Bream of Gerontius
Hake and John Dory
Ray, Cod and Haddock

In leading roles,
Ling Turbot for a tenner
The Fish Opera, Brill.
Shark, Fin Macool
Was it not
Who taught St Pirran
To make crab soup ?
With scallops for eyes.
Sea weed in hand.
Whiting to go.
It rains
Gutters work overtime.

JC

Fish Magic

Here lies the holy fish: its fading gloss
Comes off as tacky sequins on your hand.
Nothing averts its eyes of milk and glass,
Or improves the dead sourness
Of its downturned mouth.

White meat conveyed to the white tooth,
That melts in a memory of salt,
That leaves its last taste on your tongue –
But it leaps to life in a thousand
Chevrons of bone, is away
In infinite flicks of muscle,
In the only afterlife it knows,
The resurrection of numbers.

LS

Edible Child

Sleeping child
I bend to breathe your
melon-scented infant skin,
I taste the soft bloom
on your plum-skin arms,
tickle my nose on the hairs
of your gooseberry legs,
nibble your figlet toes.

Edible child
once upon a time
I heard my mother's hunger:

I love you so much
I could eat you all up.

ER

Eating Maize

From the very first it has been
a history of destructions:
the long leaves wincing,
silky tassels torn away
from buttery knuckles clenched
as tightly as a grenade.

Year after year I suck
the sweet and yellowed bone
of rich summer, teeth
burrowing inwards until
the racks are hollow, and I hold
nothing but tough litter.

Then I dream how with one
long and careful cut
I might find, inside the core,
a whole hillside crackling
with head-high plantations,
acres of solid fruit.

Supreme illusionist,
I can recreate hope
endlessly, like a set
of gleaming Russian dolls
by Caesarian section
out of a single season.

Yet from the first it was
a history of destructions:
in winter I see myself
as an old but never replete
cannibal, eating my heart out
with a terrible hunger for innocence.

LS

Capsicum Rap

Am a red, am a orange, am a yella, am a green,
when ya pull ma pin, ma seeds is snow-storm white
an' am raw in da jaw, am spittin' when ya bite,
am a red, am a orange, am a yella, am a green.

Am a green, am a yella, am a orange, am a red,
ya split me on the skillet, da fire blackenin' ma skin,
an' am soffenin' and sweetenin' like out of a tin,
am a green, am a yella, am a orange, am a red.

Am a orange, am a green, am a red, am a yella,
Am smooth in da hand, ya can stroke me, fella,
Am a pepper an' am hot, am no Cinderella,
Am a orange, am a green, am a red, am a yella.

Am a red, am a orange, am a yella, am a green,
like me, roast me, stuff me, nottin' in between,
Am the pepperest pepper ya ever been seen,
Am a red, am a orange, am a yella, am a green.

AP

Onion

Decapitate the dome, beard the chin,
strip the dry brown paper to the skin;
peel a translucent layer that swells,
each epidermis full of nuclear cells;
fry in a sweaty hot-dog, caramelise or dice,
Indian, Italian, French; or finely slice
then slowly soften in goulash; red or white,
hold the slippery crescents up to the light,
and when reduced to tears, you ought to
remember; this flavour-bomb is mostly water.

AP

Apple Haiku

Acres of blossom -
Row upon row of neat petals
Pulling them in.

>Orchards of peace
>Identify the first bite –
>Sweet taste of another world.

Juice flowing between narrow slats -
An orange waterfall
That must be tasted.

>Dark surrounds the vast barrels
>Like a secret veil –
>Months of doing its own thing.

Worth waiting for
First glass, first sip -
Squeak of a wooden tap.

>Stamped into the new cider's passport –
>Silent nod
>Quiet murmur of approval.

JC

Burrow Hill   Cider Farm

There in the barn dark | layer by layer
Inch by inch | gallon gallon
The steady inquisition | begins
The confession extracted | bit by bit
As the press pushes home | life blood of the heathen apple
Flows ever more freely | the stout cheese dripping
Ruddy brown and golden | like honey
A river in flood | a hive of fruit
Whole orchards | pulped and crushed
The never ending tide | trailers
Ebbing and flowing | acres deep and rounded
Mounds of apples | tipped and spewed forth
Like long barrows | the farm yard filled to bursting
Lagoons of red and yellow… | Brown Snout and Chisel Jersey
Dabinett and Porter's Perfection | Stoke Red and Kingston Black
Bloody Turk, Yarlington Mill | Lambrook Pippin
Tremlett's Bitter, Tom Putt | Royal Somerset
Their ransomed juice | pumped to distant vats
Vast in their yeast brooding | potent and powerful
Broad in the beam | fecund and fattening
Their froth fermenting bellies | bound with oak
Straps of iron, barrels | giant and gargantuan
A Norman trick | this drink from apples
Distilled and fiery | hint of orchard on the tongue…

JC

Green Apples

Orchard apples
acid green
twist the face in sweet distaste

Snuggled in their
porcelain bowl
shadowed curve and shining sky

Granny Smiths'
innocence
sours the tongue's experience

Seditious things
apples are
hardcore hate in skintight love

Watch out
Eve left her
dental records in this fruit.

ER

Riverford Rocket

Green sheaf of arrows,
A quiver shot from the soil
Harvested in countless veg boxes

Launch pad for a thousand salads
Shuttling into orbit with Dartmouth crab
Cornish earlies, sharp risotto

The trajectory, exotic sandwiches,
Cutting edge, re-entry, gone to seed
Spreads its wings for another year.

JC

Gathering Mushrooms at Pyhaniemi

I was perfectly happy
until you decided to tell me
about the bears:

how after glasnost
they started moving west
across the border,

these fur-coat communists
seeking fresh territory
to scent-mark.

Down in the capital
the bureaucrats are eager
to preserve wildlife

but up here people just want
to preserve their children
from being mauled,

and I just want to find
kanterelli without startling
at every broken twig

and blackened root-mass.
I'm already baffled by the
fickleness of fungus,

distracted by wild
strawberries rain-mushed
in a mesh of green,

and fallen birch leaves
cunningly disguised as the
fleshy apricot trumpets

of kanterel mushrooms
nudging their way through
moss and leaf-mould.

In the market they're saying
it's a bad year, everything
rotting before ripening,

and just as we decide
there's nothing doing today
you swoop down crying

'Halleluja!' and every bear
in the neighbourhood
takes instant flight.

ER

Paysages Moralisés 2

Grand high billows, Constable cloud
And, far beneath, an eyepiece made
From perfect hedgerows, arching trees.
Summer is a natural art, its peepshows
Aimed at infinity's parallel poles.

We look down on a hayfield pale
And razored as any in the quilted counties
Of southern England. Under the haze,
An atmospheric that the working gears
Of distant machines can hardly parse.

The car creaks as it cools. Lunch
Is exemplary, laid out inch by inch –
Fluted spring onions, carmine radishes,
Ham, lettuce, tomatoes, bread
And wine. The rug hugs the slope of the field.

The picknicker's art is deftly to fold
Past and future into the shape
Of now: in genuine hampers, to ship
The freight of leisure to the open air,
To remake Elysium from things as they are.

But try as we may, something has faltered.
No version of pastoral can filter
Justice from beauty: its silver tongue
Cannot hope to delay for long
The storm looming, the weight that has massed

Outside the frame and surely must
Burst any moment. We pack and drive straight
Back to the city. Beggars. The streets
Padlocked. Cardboard shelters. Time
Beating like a held bird, longing to fly.

LS

Aubergine

Parental Guidance is needed here.
Children have misconceived ideas
about plants, the more so when
they drop at night from the moon,
conjuring tastes to fear.

Lamps of darkness, slugs
of giant's blood,
disembodied bruises
with the squeaky plastic feel
of cheap hand-bags;

the unco-operative flesh
cuts like polystyrene,
refuses to stay white,
soaks up oil, tastes as if
it had never quite been fresh.

By far the best part
is catching them piled in baskets,
glowing darkly, whispering
of Greek islands, warm nights,
dark wine, close to the heart.

AP

The Marrow

I am peeling a marrow
flaying it with a minimalist
potato peeler
shaped like a lyre.

It strips like green and white striped
vinyl wall paper
rasps like the sharkskin tablecloths
our grandmothers used
to soften the marble

I think of the long soft whiteness of your arms

make a chisel of my fingertips
gouge out the spongy mush
hopeful with little seeds

slice glistening half-moons
into the pan
remembering
how little water a marrow needs
after its long thirst.

ER

The Meat Commission, Kenya

Beached upcountry
it rides the hills,
all cabins lit,
a frantic steamer
waving the flag
of its fine name.

Daily the cattle
replenish the ark,
nodding to their death
in a shroud of dust,
fruit of the plains'
long seasons.

And daily the knife
divides and discards:
horn and hoof
rattle down chutes,
tinned flesh
glints in the railyards.

In how many places
with fine names
have sleeves been rolled
above blood level,
even in the name
of our salvation ?

Night and day
the maribous wait
and, trembling, adore
the curdled air.
Their endless appetites
burden the trees.

                                        LS

Tripe and Cow'eels

Tuesday afternoons, if we were unlucky
and not at school, we went to Burnley market.
My gran toured us round, looking at shelves of toys,
while never buying a thing, always heading
for the sad place we dreaded- the tripe stall.
Oh, the milk-white, slippery, vinegary-ness,
the honeycomb impossibility
of eating a cow's second stomach!
The wrapped in shiny paper-ness,
the cutting and eating as if it were fish and chips;
strong tea in hospital cups, undrinkable
under the signs for Tripe and Cow Heels,
Blood Drinks, Blood Puddings…
almost as bad as the oysters of phlegm
our neighbour Jock spat on the pavement
outside our door, on his way to work.
The boakening, retching, uneatable-ness.
Years later, as guests of honour
at a Kikuyu wedding, we watched the slaughter
and disembowelling of the family's prize goat,
to then be offered the prime cut- grey, warm tripe.
No, please God, no. Not tripe.

AP

The Pie Do

This was our treat of the month.
Grandma would make a 'tatie pie
for a do at the Methodist chapel –
we were church, but we still went –
on Friday night. There'd be a turn,
a comic or a crooner, an old alto
singing G and S, maybe a whist-drive.
The women were busy back-stage –
each of their pies in heaving basins,
big enough to feed two dozen –
while us kids ran wild, and mocked
the made-up men in costume on the stage.

The interval was longer than the play.
The pastry topping came first, huge slabs;
then steaming, greyish-gravied spuds,
cooked with shin beef and a dollop of peas,
and if you were lucky, brown, bottled sauce.
The ladies – they became such when they served –
passed round the bowls and spoons.
We gobbled up, and cried for more; poor old alto.
But it wasn't so much the food;
the treat, for kids with nowhere else to go,
was simply that it was a grown-up 'do'.

AP

Mushy Peas

The 'Daily Telegraph' said the EU
had banned mushy peas. But it isn't true.
The eurocrats only put a ban
on colouring vegetables in a can.
But who wants to colour a delicacy
like the more-ish, mushed-up marrowfat pea?
Soak overnight in lots of water,
(don't be tempted by anything shorter)
cook for two hours, drain off the excess,
add butter, salt, black pepper, then press
and beat till they're mushy, with stainless steel,
(leave a few peas whole, to give it appeal).
Serving suggestion? Do you need advice?!
A slosh of malt vinegar can be nice;
but the perfect accompaniment, says I,
is a Holland's or Stanforth's hot meat pie.

AP

Schink Knodel Suppe

Langlauf lessons were a surprise;
trying and failing to stay in the ruts
(falling over can be such fun!)
in five deep feet of snow, so
we took our aching groins and thighs
back to the liegenstule huts
facing the cloudless Tyrolean sun.

The choice of soup made one think:
knodel, knodel or Schink knodel.
A bowl of oxo-tasting liquor
(we all expected it to be thicker)
mined with a bowl-sized, ticking bomb
of stale-tasting bread, milk that's curdled,
onion, egg – and lots of schink.

Knodel come in many kinds;
and many years have passed, since
peach dumplings were all there was for lunch
at the furnace factory outside Linz,
or Knedliki in Prague baroque
near the famous town hall clock
at the Two Cats – one of my finds.

I can safely say they're a fantastic treat
When you've gone for days with nothing to eat.

AP

Well Hung in the Outer Isles

Halfway to mutton and still smelling of the sea
A three year old wether, bred on heather
Finished on seaweed
Left hanging in the old black house

Down by the ghosted Hebridean shore
Slung with hook and rope
A sagging roof beam,
Beneath the fumbling thatch

Air dried in the oceanic wind
Like the cleats of St Kilda
The carcass, out of dog's range
Firm as leather, dark as peat,

Chunks sliced off when needed.
Left swinging in the evening light,
Ancient reminder of how things were:
Best sheep meat I ever tasted.

JC

Stuffing Balls

My mother is making stuffing balls, rolling
breadcrumbs, parsley and grated ham knuckle
between floured hands: her annual martyrdom.
Beyond the kitchen window one leaf like a scrap
of pumpkin flesh twirls in the cherry tree.
My brothers are nowhere to be seen, probably
out snapping icicles from the leaky gutter.
My father slinks in from the garage. 'You've been
smoking again,' my mother says (he never
knows how she knows) and brushes flour
through her hair, a frosty premonition.
This is how things are in the run-up to Christmas:
the stuffing balls, and the coming of the cold.

ER

Stew an' 'Ard Lost

Probably unheard of beyond Nelson and Colne,
or over the moors beyond Wycoller Dene,
we Barlickers made this dish our own;

Lancashire oatcake with brawn. Last seen
at Stanley's Crumpets, in Park Road.
A website pleading for help must mean

our recipe is lost. You may look abroad
in Stoke, or Leek: but their oatcakes flop.
My gran hung hers on the rack to go hard

and U-shaped, as bought from Stanley's shop.
The brawn is made from lean shoulder of pork
in a tasty jelly of veg. and trotters, chopped

with parsley, salt and pepper. You don't need a fork;
slice an onion on your stew an' 'ard,
grab it with both hands, and go to work.

As students, we'd sit at night in the yard
at the Cross Gaits, a three-mile trudge
(the only pub from which we weren't barred!)

and sluice it with pints of Burtonwood
or Thwaites, or Duttons, the local brews;
up there in the wind, it tasted bloody good.

When all that story's finished, what's the news?
(As Yeats famously asked). If Stanley's secret's
alive, I'll make you an offer you can't refuse.

AP

Wild Boar at Burrator

Snuffling the dark,
Strange tourists hugging the woods

Going south in winter
No doubt sniffed the acorns

From a great distance.
Meavy Oak Fair

On a spit. Local food.
Habeas Porcus.

JC

Ode to a Cornish Pasty

You may sink your teeth into me
Meaty morsel, croust and crib
Skirt and tatties with a touch of swede
Peppered up, crimped and folded.

Hot stuff, hoggan, convenient, fast
Baked to a turn, you can hold me close
Warm you hands on my curved body
Slide me into your pocket.

I reared the Cornish nation,
Gave men the strength they needed
Working lodes of tin and copper
Driving stope, level and adit

Faces that have eaten a thousand pasties
Stood the test of time. A family affair,
Smuggled overseas, secret recipes
Still brought to surface down under.

You may sink your teeth into me
Feel the afterglow deep inside.
Tasty reminder of creature comforts.
Lick your lips, lie back and think of Cornwall.

JC

Porcupine and Mammoth

In the Yukon dog sledging,
Uncle Theodore ate porcupine
Huskies cornered it, harnesses hung

In the trees, 'case they ate them.
Baked over the fire like hedgehog.
"Hell's Bells Sergeant, I'm twenty one."

A bit spiky, the quills singed
Camp fire cooking, but otherwise good
Better tasting than bear or wolf.

84 below and still as a whisper.
Next camp, something like beef
The nearest cow a thousand miles away.

Indian chief drew two curved lines in the snow
Like an elephant with tusks.
Land slipped, been feasting on it for a month.

The river pilots said that they could navigate
At night between the shoals, dodging the smell,
The sense of decay, ancient signposts. Landmark.

JC

Curried Squirrel

Take a brace of squirrel, grey not red
Not poisoned, better shot,
One assumes they are already dead.

You have to experiment, it is the only way
My brother brought them home
Cooked them on the Saturday.

Oriental spices wafted through the house
Coriander, cumin, turmeric and ginger
Could have been rabbit, badger or mouse.

Don't be fooled, they are a menace of course
Ruthlessly stripping bark from tree to tree,
Remove the shot, the secret is in the sauce.

JC

Turnip

No wonder they're reduced.
Do we eat them any more?
Aren't they fodder for beasts,
or the rural poor?

The Scots know better:
it may sound risky,
but haggis and neeps
are brilliant with whisky.

They're buttery-soft
In a slow-cooked lamb curry;
Deep, blushing pebbles.
Go on, buy some; don't worry!

AP

sow   grow
pick   quick
chop   crop
pack stack
store more
nice price
plastic
drastic
no panic
organic
long
strong
blue
hue
green
sheen
bright
white
bite
squeak
squeak
leek

AP

Raspberries

Small red hand grenades
Hiding beneath the camouflage
Their fragmentation
Defused and plucked

Their flavours exploding
Within the mouth
The wounds
A tell tale line around the lips.

JC

Cooking Damsons

Deep red, purple red, emperor red
Stewing around, a vast vat of dye

Bubbling, oozing their small stones
Pipped to perfection, flesh opening up

Tart and sharp, they sell themselves readily
By wayside shrines. On the game

So much a pound, a punnet, a box
The season is short, but the memory is long

Last summer jammed into a Kilner jar.
Decadent, debauched, pickled in Vodka.

JC

Sloes

No lack of present wonders –
the rowan's star-showers
stopped with blood,
the polished ochre
of acorns, some
clamped in their cups,
or the pungent sapwood
locked into each tight bead of holly.

But the darkest amazements of all
in the bright scour
of autumn riches
are the sloes that hang
among wicked spines,
their blue-black skin
misted with a bloom
like breath staying on a flawless mirror.

Cutting one open, you find
a simple pulp
of greeny yellow,
weak moonlight,
and a single nubble
bedded in blister-water,
a bone-hard core,
an oubliette that beggars belief.

From somewhere, the purest birdsong –
last flarings
of the cherished light.
Always you return
to the sloe, to test
the coinage, to conjure
from its sour heart
the future perfect of its white flowers.

LS

Mangoes

You may find them

hung like Christmas baubles
in the Venda trees,

piled as green pyramids
in Karatina market,

bound in palm baskets
on the streets of Mombasa,

boxed for export
along Rockey Street,

bussed in bucket-loads
from Shai-Shai to Maputo,

soft and sucky
by Srinagar temples,

wrinkled and yellow
on Whitechapel Road,

turned inside out
and hedgehogged, for children:

And always, always,
The flesh that cuts like liver,
Soft, yet stringy in the teeth;

the yellow of Buddhist saffron,
perfume of Zanzibar nights
along a mangrove shore,

drowning in jasmine
under these Lamu stars.

                                        AP

Riddle

Once, in the steady shade of my tree,
the unicorn sat with the pale lady:
now among the Christmas lights
my airy ghosts gleam in the night.

Strangely inverted, their polar crowns
are north not south, up not down:
they lack my burnish of red and gold,
the paradise seed I'm said to hold.

One equatorial cut reveals
me as I am, two pip-crammed star-wheels:
and then, my bitter smell of wood,
thin juice like water mixed with blood.

Held by the infant Christ, I weigh
life longer than the length of days:
a symbol to outflank grey stone,
a riddle solved by faith alone.

LS

Wild Strawberries

The little fruits wink
in the light like
scarlet beads rolled
from a broken thread.

Sometimes three or four
to a slender stem
and not where you might
expect to find them,

sweetening in the sun,
but in a birch wood
secretive in a green
serrated leaf den

among grasses tall
as a boy turning man.
I pick greedily,
remembering how

once upon a time
we swore not love
but allegiance, pressed
thumb to cut thumb,

sucking blood berries
and tasting iron. Later,
pulsing on the screen
of my closed eyes,

the red-breasted bird
beckons from the forest,
the sharp spindle stains
snow white rose red.

ER

White Peach

Under the skin,
itself rose soft
but tough, bitter,
the flesh, firm
yet tender
to the knife,
dense with sugars

The flesh, white
not yellow,
white at the border
of green, the colour
of iceberg roses,
with the pallor of illness
at its most alluring

Long before
you reach the stone-heart
with its hard ridges,
you will be up
to your elbows
in runnels of juice,
your fingers dripping

And memory, turned
informer, will tell
that you know already
this bitter-sweetness
you fear and desire –
the linger of it
on your drenched lips

LS

A Dales Dessert

A nice bit of Wensleydale
from the Hawes Creamery,
(saved from extinction
by Wallace and Gromit);
silky-dry, firm,
more crumbly than Cheshire,
less messy, less acid
than Lancashire. Of course.

Eaten in wedges
On brick-shaped chunks
of rich, moist cake,
currant-full, claggy,
sherry-scented, dark
as Christmas pudding,
Mars-bar sweet to the so slight
sour of the cheese. Please!

You with the delicate palate,
you so sophis', what lack
of heart and taste,
excess of prejudice.
Stay mystified for life.
This is the Dales' dessert,
formidable, not debased,
too good to waste. On you.   AP

Blue Vinny

White and blue, crumbly mould
That slips between the cheese wire,
Truckles about the size of cartwheel hubcaps

Hand skimmed and harnessed, the morning's milk
A sidekick of butter making,
The story rumbling on in meadows

Measureless to man and beast
The slow pace of the herd, rich blue veins
Spreading out across the Blackmore Vale.

JC

Hard Cheese Somerset

On the shelf, breathing gently
Acres of grass swaddled in muslin,
Cloaked and clothed, the milk's residue,

A pressing engagement
Turned and turned again
Wheels of cheddar,

Itching to go.
The flavour of each farm
Trapped, encased in rind

A sharp reminder of nature's
Temperamental ways,
The real farmhouse pulling you back

Tradition unpasteurized
The price of keeping pace
With the herd's yield.

Another year measured out in tons,
A 'hands on' operation
That binds the cheddar to the land.

JC

Pistachios and Mussels

Age by colour and in wrinkles:
The withheld, the clitoral,
The green of a vivid sapling,
The orange-grey of nothing else.

The secret that must be prised
Or bitten apart;
Analogies, if any,
By rhyme – gloss, loss:
The body, the heart.

LS

Devon Cream Tea

First find your tea shop
Laden with horse brasses,
Or better still make your own
At home sweet home.

Clotted and chunky, the yellow
Raw material scooped up
Scalded and allowed to settle
Over night and then spread

With vigour, not forgetting
The butter and strawberry jam
Red and yellow traffic lights
On the green grass

The rug spread out
Like a Kashmir shawl
Dotted with scones and splits
Like mountain peaks

Avalanches at every turn.
Off piste you can lick
Your fingers and savour
The cream's cleavage.

JC

The Hostess Trolley

I can't bear anything luke-warm, she said

He took a van to Merthyr Tydfil
It's a bargain, they said

It was all chrome and walnut veneer
And the rear off-side wheel
Had a slight wobble

Just what I always wanted, she said

He dabbed balsamic on each pulse
Cleaned his fingernails with fresh dough
Ground spices from the east
Between his teeth

We hope we're not too early, they said

He wheeled her in
Pan-fried hostess in her own jus
Piping hot.

ER

Dorset Knobs

Caught between a rock and a hard place
They live forever, their sell by date
Several centuries hence, an advantage

If you were out on the Grand Banks
Or simply pruning trees, or set in the top
Of a mug of tea, with raw egg, furmity almost.

                                                    JC

Valentine's Night in the Supermarket

Goodbye hope to see you again soon
All night the unspoken words
track across the screens
of the checkouts – all retail romances
demand that goodbye is hello,
that shopping is what goes on
happily ever after
hope to see you

All is well, beneath
the unblinking harvest lights –
the meats are covered with paper,
the shelves restocked, thousands
of gleaming bottles rub shoulders,
plenty walks down the aisles
see you again

Here all noise has been channelled
into ducts, or the phlegmy dozing
of constant refrigeration,
here is the world in a chain
of brands, of air-freighted seasons,
each place a clone of everywhere
again soon

You must not think that gorse
is out of bloom, that anyone
is sobbing in a corner, afraid
that kissing is out of season,
or that something has been forgotten
though endlessly repeated
soon goodbye hope
Goodbye hope to see you again soon

LS

Eight Failed Recipes For Preserving Love

'Give me love,' I said, intent on preservation:
you gave it willingly, mindful only of the present.

I drenched it in exotic syrups till it crystallised:
'Too cloying,' you said, wiping your sugared lips.

I soused it in vinegar and hot bruised spices:
still a filmy pale mould crept in from the edges.

I rubbed sea salt between its fleshy layers:
you complained that it stung like iodine on a graze.

I froze it in straw bedded deep in a sullen cave:
you dug out the shrunken core, trampled the ooze.

I pegged it like Baltic herring on a desolate shore:
'It will rot,' you said, watching the weather vane swing.

I bottled it, set it sealed and labelled on a shelf.
'Do you remember frogs in formaldehyde?' you asked.

I shrouded it in smoke from smouldering fevers:
you dreamed of your mother in the crematorium.

I smoothed it with oils of perpetuity:
'It smells of death,' you said, your eyes swivelling.

ER

Sad Cake

Well it weren't cake,
and it weren't sad.
It were flat and round
and it didn't taste bad.
A Lancashire thing.

Best buttered when warm
before it got hard,
it were basically flour,
currants and lard.
A just-baked thing.

The bits left over
(all crumbly and cold)
went into your snap tin.
It were sometimes weeks old.
A weaver's thing.

Me dad always said
It were better than scone,
Because scones had two bottoms.
And since he's gone,
It's a history thing.

AP

A few Somerset Recipes to get your head round make your mouth water… whet the appetite

Whortleberry jelly, Syllabub and Mead,
Eggiot, Possett and Elderberry wine

Tansy, Beestings and Frumenty
Herby Pie and Elder Flower fritters

Sucking Pig and Forced cabbage,
Pork Cheese and Sheep's head,

Pig's head, Lamb's tail and brawn
White Hunting Stew and Muggety pie

Poor Man's Goose and Mutton sausages
Rook pie, jugged hare and devilled sardines

Samphire hash and mock turtle soup
Elver loaf and Carnival pudding

Loganberry flummery, Pears in junket
Dough boys and pigeon breasts

Shrimp toast and rabbit mould
Zinch pie and smoked conger

Fennel tea and Lovage soup
Pond pudding and blackberry cobbler

Apple liver and Bath chaps
Laver salad, Icky pie and Roast gliny

Sloe gin and Wassail Punch
Linseed tea and mangold wine.

Wallfish and herring pie
Whit pit, faggots and ham.

JC

Decision

After dinner which consisted of polenta,
roasted cod on a bed of chickpea mush
and lemon geranium cake with organic wine

I picked up an attractive programme
that advertised a weekend of green cuisine
and a special course on women's health:

I would learn how to eat for well-being
radiance and vitality in three days
at the genuine mediaeval organic centre where

I was promised juice followed by yoga
before breakfast and a talk on preventing
osteoporosis, followed by a break;

there would be morning and afternoon
demonstrations of dishes to enhance
natural menopause and discourage cancer;

all foods would be rich in phytosterols
and there would be lunch and questions
before departure. I decided not to go.

ER

Honey with Sir Kenelm Digby

The Honey of dry open Countries,
where there is much Wild-thyme,
Rosemary, and Flowers is best.

It is of three sorts, Virgin-honey,
Life-honey, and Stock-honey.
The first is best. The Life-honey next.

The Virgin-honey is of Bees,
that swarmed the Spring before ,
And are taken up in Autumn;

and is made best by chusing
the Whitest combs of the Hive,
and letting the Honey run out of them

lying upon a Sieve without pressing it,
or breaking of the Combs.
The Life-honey is of the same Combs

broken after the Virgin-honey is run from it:
The Merchants of Honey do use
to mingle all the sorts together.

The first of a swarm is called Virgin-honey.
That of the next year, after the Swarm
has hatched, is Life-honey.

And ever after, it is Honey of Old-stocks.
Honey that is forced out of the Combs,
will always taste of Wax.

JC

Feeding the Dolls

The two year olds
are feeding their dolls
air sandwiches
crammed with promises –
and brought at a run
from the bright kitchen
endlessly stocked
with imagination
and their delight.

The dolls are sitting
in bloated collapse,
stomachs out,
heads hanging –
as over-full
as the hog flung
down from the ramparts
of Carcassonne
to show besiegers
that there really was
food to spare
in the suffering city.

LS

A Cautionary Tail

Pork and Bacon
Scratching a living

In cider dealing
In cider information

The big bad apple
Rotten to the core

The piggy bank
Bringing home the bacon

The trough, a small depression
In which is placed your casserole

Normally of course we talk
Of having it on a plate, beefing it up,

Spoon fed titbits of information
She put him out to grass

Milking the system
A bread and butter letter

Creaming off the subsidies
The hot potato

Butter wouldn't melt in his mouth
Led by the nose, the herd instinct

Bullish, thinking on the hoof
The apple tart,

She had it on a plate
Pig in the middle

The apple of his eye
Mutton dressed up as lamb

He made a meal of it.
His stag party

Chewing the cud
On the horns of a dilemma

Ramming it home
Fleeced again, cheesed off

He chickened out
A bun in the oven

The sauce of all good things
The suite taste of success

Sir Loin for the chop.
Like a lamb to slaughter

She had him over a barrel
Farmed out, penned up

There's a good Bath chap.
His rump, bringing up the rear.

Mucking out
The Gateway to success

Bread is the Staff of Life
But Cider is life itself.

Move over Rover.
Biscuits for you and biscuits for I

She took the lot.
Silver side or brisket

A hiding to nothing
Ox tail at last.

JC

Notes

Cornish Earlies. The Golden Mile is an area of land behind Mounts Bay where the earliest potatoes grow. They are in fact grown all over the south coast of Penwith from Sennen to Helston and traditionally were eaten with pilchards. Varieties include Rocket, Lady Crystal, Premiere, Maris Peer, Riviera and Alchemira. The real season runs from late April to early June. Beware cheap imitations out of season…

Fast Food – Low Tide. Glatting was carried out within living memory on the Somerset Coast around Kilve. Not sure if this is covered by the new legislation on hunting with dogs… Mud-horses are the wooden sledges that are pushed out over the mud to check the stake nets off Stolford. The story is that several centuries ago the landowners, the Luttrells were asked how far their rights went and they said they went out 'as far their horse could ride' so they re-named the sledges 'mud horses' to extend their fishing rights right out to half a mile and of course ensured their income from fishing dues. Laver was sent up to London from Somerset in the 19th century.

Elvers. Elvers are a very Somerset dish but are rarely eaten now. They are often sold for restocking of rivers and are also exported to China for growing-on into eels for sushi for the Japanese market. The price of elvers can vary from £50–£250 a kilo depending on the market and the quality. Sadly, they are now appear to be in decline. The elver season is from March to May. Elvers are spawned in the Sargasso and are brought over on the Gulf Stream. They are two or three years-old when they arrive in the Parrett and the Severn Estuary.

Sea Bass. The beach was the Hive at Burton Bradstock and the Rana jointly owned with Simon Eastwood. The bass was bought by Arthur Watson for his Restaurant the Riverside Café at West Bay. A novel use for the Post Office scales. The price then was £4 a pound.

Burrow Hill Cider Farm. This poem has been split using the 'Anglo Saxon' mid line break as a device for splitting two voices and even for making two separate poems, like cleaving hazel, each side mirroring the other. Something Seamus Heaney alluded to in his translation of Beowulf.

Mushy Peas. Holland's famous pies are made in Baxenden, East Lancashire. Stanforth's Celebrated Pork Pie Shop is in Skipton, North Yorkshire. Being born right on the border, of a Lancashire mother and a Yorkshire father, I have to be impartial!

Schink Knodel Suppe. *Liegenstule* are deck-chairs.

Well Hung in the Outer Hebrides. In the 1970s I lived for a year in the Outer Hebrides and the crofters were incredibly generous. In Uig, Lewis, they often used their abandoned half-fallen-in 'black houses' as an outdoor larder. The meat was superb, being a cross between the Black-face and the local Hebridean. A wether is of course a castrated ram lamb that is allowed to grow on. In the Hebrides, sheep have a penchant for sea weed and can swim quite long distances. Preserving meat without a freezer is an art all of its own.

Stew an' 'Ard Lost. Barlickers are residents of 'Barlick', officially called Barnoldswick.

Wild Boar at Burrator. In 2005-6 wild 'wild boar' have been very much on the menu of the media and have been spotted all over Devon and Dorset. Some escaped of their own accord, others were let out by fringe elements of the animal rights brigade. In 2005, wild boar were even hunted with dogs, unsuccessfully, on the edge of Exmoor.

Porcupine and Mammoth. Uncle Theodore joined the North West Mounted Police after the Boer War and went up to the Yukon. He spent two years there and became good friends with the poet Robert Service and often took Service down town to the red-light district of Whitehorse, and then back to their canteen where he gleaned their stories from coming off patrol. Patrols in winter were three weeks at a time with a dogs and sledges. Lonely but fantastic. Frozen mammoth was not that unusual. Wolves were a problem and he had a narrow escape with a bear. Caribou wasn't bad either.

Curried Squirrel. At the age of 16 my brother whilst still at school was an apprentice gamekeeper and was always experimenting with food that he had shot. This was in 1970, long before it was fashionable to eat local food…

Mangoes. If the two sides are cut off, criss-crossed with a knife and turned inside out, it becomes a 'hedgehog'.

Blue Vinny. Blue Vinny is the true cheese of Dorset and derives its name from 'veinney' meaning veined. In Dorset there is at least one Vinney Cross and a Veinney Pond. The art of making the cheese died out in the late 1960s Occasionally it surfaced as out-of-date Stilton and there was much secrecy and rumour about its existence. Commercial production restarted at Stock Gaylard in 1985. It should be made from unpasteurized milk and was often used as a way of using up excess milk in times of glut. A wine merchant on the Danube near Budapest in Hungary once informed me that Blue Vinny was the best accompaniment for Tokay.

Devon Cream Tea. Selling Cornish and Devon cream teas was illegal during the Second World War and secret locations were often whispered by word of mouth. The real enigma. Remote farms at the end of tracks. A favourite destination for honeymooning couples… Cornish is with splits then jam with cream on top. Devon is with splits or chudleighs, cream and then jam. Cream is of course clotted. The real test is to turn the tub or jar upside down and it won't fall out.

Dorset Knobs. Dorset Knobs are still made at Morecombelake in West Dorset and are often used as an accompaniment for Blue Vinny. They are very hard... dentures beware.

Honey with Sir Kenelm. *The Closet of the Eminently Learned Sir Kenelme Digbie Kt. Opened* (1669). His young and beautiful wife Venetia died of a surfeit of viper's broth on May Day 1633 and with characteristic style Sir Kenelm summons Van Dyck to do a portrait... His book edited by Jane Stevenson and Peter Davidson was reprinted by Prospect Books in 1997 and is masterpiece of observation and culinary inquisitiveness. A sweetener.

Gathering mushrooms and **wild strawberries** is a summer activity in Finland, in my case at a delicious summer place called Pyhaniemi, on a lake near a small town called Juva.

The cover illustration

The front cover, with its four fishes (symbolizing the four poets) shows, from the top, a tail of a porbeagle shark, a tail of a monk or angel fish and then two sunfish, swimming in opposite directions. The copper plate is from original drawings taken on the spot in Mount's Bay by Mr Jago in May 1743. The sunfish was caught and landed in Penzance. The plate is reproduced from *The Natural History of Cornwall* by William Borlase, AM, FRS, Rector of Ludgvan. It was published in 1758 in Oxford, printed for the author by W. Jackson.

William Borlase (1695–1772) was a learned clergyman, naturalist and antiquary. He was born in Pendeen and educated at Exeter College, Oxford. In 1722 he arrived in Ludgvan as rector and in 1732 he obtained the vicarage of St Just. He became fascinated by mining and mineral deposits and collected many fossils. In 1750 he was made a Fellow of the Royal Society and in 1754, he published, at Oxford, his *Antiquities of Cornwall.* His extensive fossil collections were presented to the Ashmolean Museum in Oxford. He received the thanks of the University and the degree of LL.D. William Borlase was well acquainted with many leading literary men of the time, particularly with Alexander Pope, with whom he kept up a long correspondence, and for whose grotto at Twickenham he furnished the greater part of the fossils and minerals. His books on Cornwall are invaluable masterpieces of observation.